PUBLIC

Dream To Win – Olympic Gold

DREAM TO WIN

Michael Phelps

Roy Apps

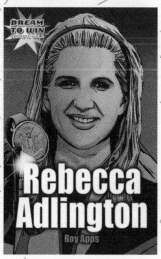

DREAM TO WIN

Rebecca Adlington

Roy Apps

978 0 7496 9028 1   978 0 7496 9195 0

Other titles in the series:

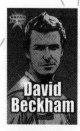

DREAM TO WIN

David Beckham

DREAM TO WIN

Lewis Hamilton

DREAM TO WIN

Hope Powell

Monty Panesar

Andy Murray

Roy Apps

978 0 7496 8232 3   978 0 7496 9027 4

First published in 2009 by
Franklin Watts
338 Euston Road
London NW1 3BH

Franklin Watts Australia
Level 17/207 Kent Street
Sydney NSW 2000

Text © Roy Apps 2009
Illustrations © Chris King 2009
Cover design by Peter Scoulding

A CIP catalogue record for this book
is available from the British Library.

ISBN: 978 0 7496 9196 7

Dewey Classification: 796.62'092

1 3 5 7 9 10 8 6 4 2

Printed in Great Britain

Franklin Watts is a division of Hachette Children's Books,
an Hachette UK company.
www.hachette.co.uk

DREAM TO WIN
OLYMPIC GOLD

Chris Hoy

Roy Apps

Illustrated by Chris King

EDGE FRANKLIN WATTS

LONDON•SYDNEY

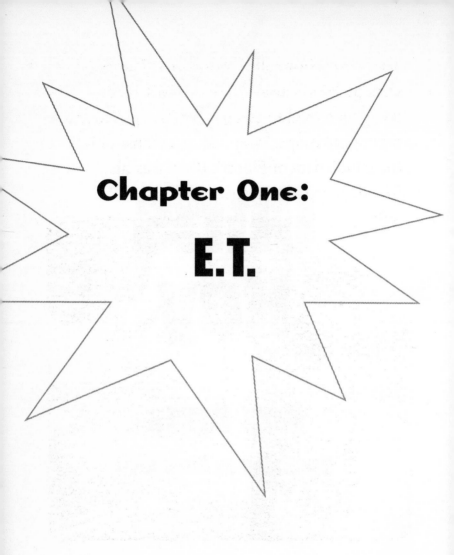

Chapter One:

E.T.

Edinburgh's largest cinema was packed with people, but nobody moved a muscle. Everyone's eyes were fixed on the giant screen. The film had nearly finished.

The hero, a boy called Elliott, and his friends were pedalling away on their BMX bikes, trying like mad to escape from the police and other grown ups. Wrapped in a blanket on the handlebars of Elliott's BMX was his friend, an extra terrestrial alien called E.T.

Just when it looked as if Elliott and his friends would be caught, they put on an extra spurt. Then, suddenly, they took off and were flying through the air on their bikes with E.T. the extra-terrestrial alien was them!

Down on the ground, the adults cursed and shook their fists as they watched the convoy of colourful BMX bikes being ridden across the sky, silhouetted by a bright, full moon.

A great cheer went up from the cinema audience.

Every kid in the world who saw the film *E.T. The Extra-Terrestrial* wanted to be a BMX rider like Elliott and his mates. The group of friends from Edinburgh, Scotland, who had gone to see the film was no different.

They walked home discussing ways to get their parents to buy them all BMX bikes, including the tallest of them, a blond boy, whose name was Chris Hoy.

Chapter Two:

The £5 Bike

"Mum, I need a BMX bike," Chris announced as soon as he got home.

"Chris, you don't need a BMX bike, you want one," replied his mother. "There is a difference you know."

"But, Mum," Chris protested, "how can I
be the best BMX rider ever, if I haven't got
a bike?"

"OK," sighed Chris's mum. "I'll see what we
can do. But your dad and I aren't made of
money, you know."

The prices of new bikes in the shops were more than Chris's mum and dad could afford. Then, one Saturday afternoon when she was at a jumble sale, Chris's mum saw a BMX bike for £5. She bought it.

Chris's dad stripped down the bike, painted it black and put new BMX stickers and handlebars on it. He was very proud of his work.

"Now, you will look after it, son, won't you?" he said.

"Course I will, Dad!" replied Chris.

After a few weeks, Chris snapped the frame by doing too many jumps off ramps made from planks of wood. The £5 bike was only good for scrap metal. He got another second-hand bike and bent the frame on that one, too.

If he was to get anywhere with BMX-ing, Chris knew he needed a proper, new, bike. He also knew the exact bike. It was a Raleigh Super Burner BMX and it cost £99. He told his dad.

"Are you serious about this BMX biking thing?" Chris's dad asked him.

"Yes! I want to be a champion bike rider one day," Chris said.

"OK," said Chris's dad, "here's what we'll do. Your mum and I will pay for half the bike, if you can raise the money for the other half."

"Thanks, Dad," said Chris excitedly.

Chris knew it was great that his parents could give him £50 towards the bike, but where could he get hold of the other £49?

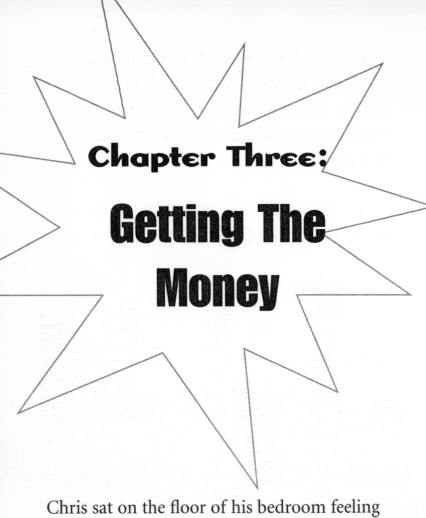

Chapter Three:

Getting The Money

Chris sat on the floor of his bedroom feeling very fed up. Even if he saved up every penny of his pocket money, it would still be months before he could afford his BMX. He looked around at all his books and toys. He'd be lucky to get 49p for the lot at a boot sale, let alone £49.

There were *Beano* annuals with torn pages, broken Action Men, jigsaws with bits missing ... all Christmas presents from his many aunties and uncles. Suddenly, Chris had an idea.

"That's it!" he said to himself, "I may not have much money, but I do have lots of relations!"

Every time his mum and dad had people round for dinner, Chris made sure to put in an appearance.

He waited until the meal was almost over – by then the guests had drunk quite a bit of wine and were feeling in a good mood. He went up to them and in an excited voice told them all about his BMX-ing. His aunties and uncles were very impressed. Then Chris's face suddenly changed and he looked very sad.

"I need a Raleigh Super Burner," he'd explain with a sigh. "Mum and Dad will pay for half, but I've got to raise £49 myself."

His aunties and uncles felt sorry for him.

"It's great you're so enthusiastic about your hobby," they said and then slipped him some money.

In no time at all Chris had the money he needed for a Raleigh Super Burner.

Chris made a great start as a BMX racer with the Edinburgh club: Danderhall Wolves. There was no doubt that he was good. Soon, he was entering weekend races all over England too.

It was tough, though. Edinburgh, Scotland is a long way from most English towns and cities.

On a Saturday before a race, Chris went to bed early; at about eight o'clock. Then his dad woke him at about one o'clock in the morning. Still half asleep he would clamber into the back of the family's big old estate car, where his dad had made up a foam mattress bed. Then he'd curl up and get another five hours' sleep, before waking at dawn in a strange English town, ready for a day's BMX racing.

Soon, Chris was the king of Scottish BMX-ing. He was getting better and better, in England too. If he did well, he didn't go hyper. If he was beaten, he didn't sulk. He just sat down with his dad and discussed the race, lap by lap.

"Next year, son," said his dad. "I reckon you could be the top BMX rider of all." Then he sighed. "But to do that, you need a really good bike. One that will cost more money than your mum and I have and certainly more than you could ever hope to scrounge off your aunties and uncles."

"How can I become a champion BMX rider," Chris thought sadly, "if I can't even afford a decent bike?"

Chapter Four:

BMX King

Chris thought about his problem and then made a decision: he would persuade somebody with lots of money that he was a future champion BMX rider in the making. He would find himself a sponsor. Chris knew that one of the most successful companies in Edinburgh was Kwik Fit, the tyres and exhausts fitters. The man who owned Kwik Fit was called Tom Farmer, and Chris reckoned he must be very rich.

In his very best handwriting, he wrote to Tom Farmer asking for sponsorship. Soon after, he got a reply: Tom Farmer wanted to meet him.

Chris and his dad went along to Tom Farmer's office.

"I've been with Chris at all his races," his dad began, "he's very talented, very keen and very committed."

"I'm sure he is, Mr Hoy," replied Tom Farmer. "But the letter I've got here is from Chris. I want to hear from him."

Chris told Tom Farmer all about his dream of becoming a top rider. When he had finished, Tom Farmer took out his cheque book and wrote Chris a cheque for £1,000. The money would go towards buying a top-of-the-range BMX bike and help Chris with all the other expenses involved in BMX racing.

Chris trained hard on his new bike. After each race, he analysed what had gone well and what had gone badly. He worked at the things he needed to do to be faster than the others: to be a champion. He practised his starts; twice a week, every week. He learned how to pace himself. By the end of the 1991 season, when Chris was fifteen, he was Scottish Champion, ranked number two in Britain and number nine in the world.

After just one more season, Chris became British number one!

Chapter Five:

Decision Time

Then, all of a sudden, the BMX bike craze had died.

There were no more BMX bikes being made or sold. There were no more races.

A new bike had appeared to replace the BMX: the MTB, or mountain bike.

Chris liked the look of the new mountain bikes. He was a champion BMX rider, so he thought it would be no trouble for him to become a champion mountain bike rider.

He pounded up hillsides and splashed through muddy streams on his new mountain bike. But with every race and time trial there were always riders faster than him.

Finally, Chris had to admit the truth. He wasn't that good at racing mountain bikes. He loved bikes, but he definitely didn't want to take part in races just for the sake of it. He wanted to be a winner! At the moment, he was far away from that.

At school though, he was showing that he was a good rugby player – he'd even captained the Edinburgh Schools Under 15's. He was an even better rower, winning a silver medal at the British Championship in the junior coxless pairs.

So Chris Hoy put his bike away and switched to rugby and rowing.

But he wasn't happy. He missed riding. At weekends and in the holidays, if he wasn't rowing or playing rugby, he took his bike out of the garage and pedalled up the hills. He even signed up for a ten-day cycling holiday with his school.

Eventually, Chris decided to sit down with his mum and dad to work out why he found mountain biking so difficult. It wasn't the biking bit, he was good at that. So, it had to be the mountains. Finally, they realised that was it! The problem was his power-to-weight ratio. Chris was tall, bulky and well-built, which is great for racing, rowing or playing rugby; but not so great for endurance sports, like mountain biking.

Chris's dad had an idea. He took his son along to the Dunedin Cycling Club in Edinburgh, which was run by Ray Harris. Ray Harris introduced Chris to track cycling. Ray Harris, like Chris, was interested in the science of cycling. He tested and experimented to find ways of becoming a better rider.

Ray Harris taught Chris how to keep a training diary and talked to him about the importance of setting goals for himself.

"That's easy," said Chris. "I know my goal. I want to be an Olympic track Champion."

But once again, Chris found he wasn't quite good enough. He was fast, but he wasn't great at moving between the racers. That meant he often found himself penned against the rails, unable to get away from the pack. Unable to win.

Then, one day in 1996, Chris was racing at the Meadowbank Velodrome in Edinburgh, and in one horrific moment, everything changed.

Chapter Six:

The Crash

The Meadowbank Velodrome had been built
in the 1970s. It was very old and made of
wood. The riders were coming up to the last
bend when the rider in front of Chris swung
slightly to one side. Chris caught his back
wheel and went down.

The riders behind piled into him, including
a young English rider called Jason Queally.
When Jason crashed, he went right over the
top, landing on his back. He screamed with
pain and slid down the wooden track.

It was obvious Jason was hurt, but nobody
realised just how badly until they went down
to him. Sticking out of his chest was a jagged
piece of broken track 45 centimetres long.
It had come right through his back. Chris's
mum was on first aid duty at the stadium
that day. She was a nurse and looked after
Jason until the ambulance arrived.

Chris was badly shaken by the accident. He kept thinking about it again and again in his mind. Watching Jason tumble through the air, seeing him crash onto the wooden planks, hearing him screaming in pain. Again, Chris wondered if cycle racing was worth it, or if it would be better for him to turn to another, safer, sport.

After a week in intensive care, Jason began to make a slow recovery from his horrific injuries. One thing was certain, Chris thought, you wouldn't ever see him on a racing bike again.

But that was where Chris was wrong.

Some months after the dreadful accident, word got round that Jason Queally had been seen out on a bike!

It seemed that although he had decided not to take part in any more group races, Jason was going to continue in individual cycling events, racing against the clock.

If Jason could carry on racing, thought Chris, then so can I.

Chapter Seven:

Olympics

Chris knew that if he was going to be a champion track cyclist, he would need top facilities. So, in 1999, he moved to Manchester where a new state-of-the-art velodrome had just been built.

That year, the cycling World Cup took place in Berlin. The other British team members were Craig Maclean and…Jason Queally. The team was not expected to do very well. In the 1998 European Championships they had finished down in tenth place.

But Chris and the sprint team had other ideas. In the final, they rode the race of their lives against the top French team. The British team won the silver medal – Britain's first sprint medal for 39 years!

After the World Cup, the team was given a professional coach for the first time. Just in time to start training for the 2000 Sydney Olympics. At the Olympics, Chris and the British sprint team won silver again. Chris was thrilled. It was his first Olympic medal.

The last team event was over. Now it was the turn of the individual riders. Chris was up in the stands cheering on the British cyclist in the 1 kilometre time trial: who was none other than Jason Queally. The favourite to win the competition was Frenchman, Arnaud Tourant. He was an awesome racer and was already World Champion.

Chris knew that Jason had prepared himself well for this race. But even he was amazed by the speed that Jason flew round the track. When his time was flashed up on the screen it read: 1 min. 1.609 seconds. A new Olympic record! Maybe, Chris thought, Jason could win silver!

The Frenchman's turn came. He cycled hard, tucking down over his handlebars and roaring round the track. When his time was flashed up it read: 1 min. 2.9 seconds. Incredibly, Jason had won the gold medal!

After all the celebrations were over, Chris strolled back to his room. He was thinking quietly to himself.

"If, after such a horrific crash, Jason has found the strength and commitment to take an individual Olympic Gold, why shouldn't I?"

So there and then he fixed his mind on the next target. He would become a champion in an individual cycling event at the next Olympics, at Athens in 2004.

The dream was on.

Fact file
Chris Hoy

 Full name: Christopher Andrew Hoy

 Born: Edinburgh, Scotland, 23 March 1976

1983-90	Aged 7–14: Races BMX: becoming Scottish Champion, British No. 2, European No. 5 and World No. 9.
1992	Joins first cycling club: Dunedin CC. Competes in mountain bike, time trials, road and track racing.
1994	Joins the Edinburgh Racing Club to concentrate on track racing.
1996	Becomes a member of the GB National Squad.
1999	World Championships Berlin: Silver medal, Team Sprint.
2000	World Cup: Silver medal, Team Sprint (British Record). Olympic Games, Sydney: Silver Medal, Team Sprint (British Record).
2002	World Cup: Gold medal, 1km Time Trial; Gold medal, Team Sprint.
2004	Olympic Games, Athens: Gold medal, 1km track time trial (Olympic Record, British Record).
2006	World Championships: World Champion, 1km Time Trial. Commonwealth Games: Bronze medal, 1km Time Trial; Gold Medal, Team Sprint.
2007	World Cup: Silver medal, Team Sprint; Gold medal, 1km Time Trial; Gold medal Keirin.
2008	Olympic Games, Beijing: 3 Gold medals, Team Sprint, Keirin and Match Sprint (Olympic Record); BBC Sports Personality of the Year.
2009	Knighted in the Queen's New Year Honours' list.

Andy Murray

The Great Britain Under-16 tennis team had done really well. They'd reached the finals of the European Team Championships.

But now they had lost their match to Spain. Most of the players weren't too depressed about their loss.

Only one member of the team looked really fed up. He didn't like losing. Especially not finals. He had a dream of becoming a top world-class player. His name was Andy Murray.

**Continue reading this story in
DREAM TO WIN: Andy Murray**

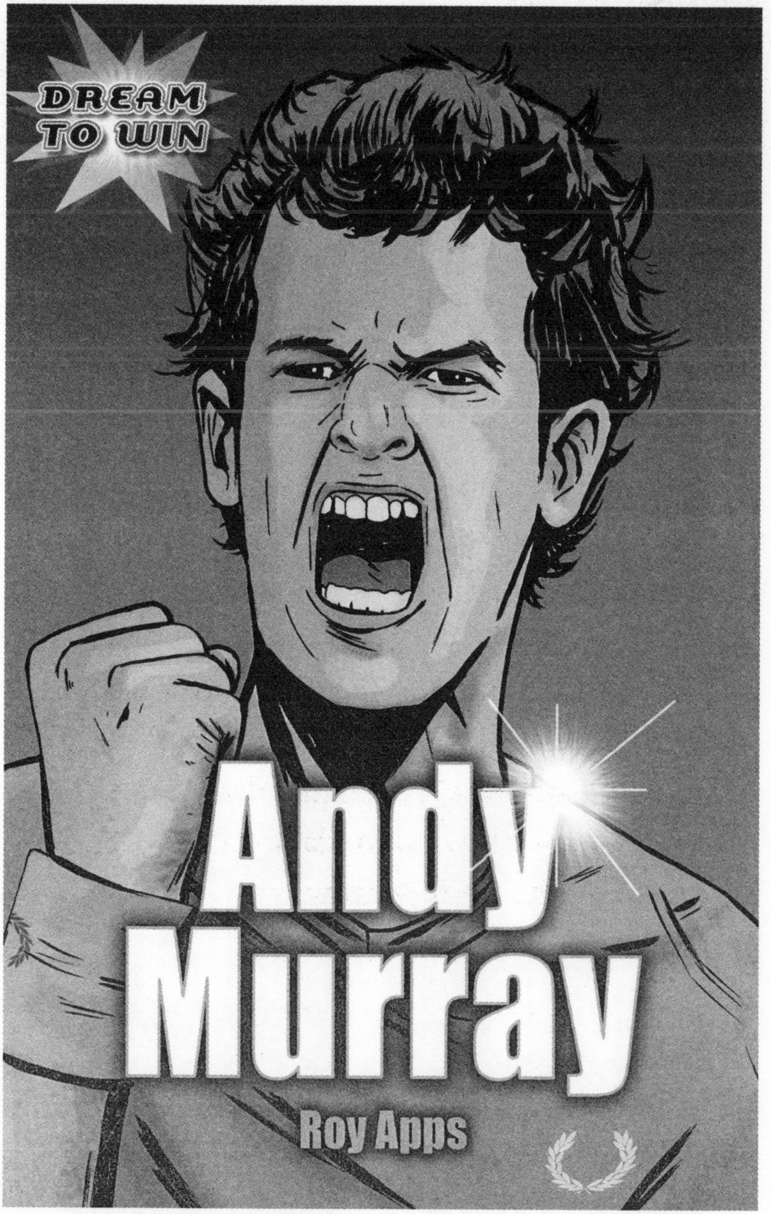
DREAM TO WIN
Andy Murray
Roy Apps

Also by Roy Apps,
published by Franklin Watts:

978 0 7496 7057 3

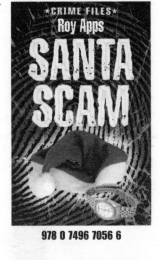

978 0 7496 7056 6

978 0 7496 7054 2

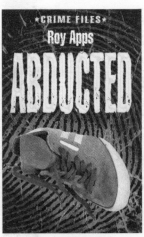

978 0 7496 7053 5